*Under Milk Wood*

*Dylan Thomas*

# Under Milk Wood

A PLAY FOR VOICES

Prefaces (1954 and 1974) by
DANIEL JONES

LONDON

J M DENT & SONS LTD

*Under Milk Wood* was first broadcast by the B.B.C. on 25 January 1954. It was presented on the stage in the tenth Edinburgh Festival in 1956 and extracts from it were shown on B.B.C. television. The stage production, by Douglas Cleverdon and Edward Burnham, of the play was given at the New (now Albery) Theatre, London, in 1956. The film of the play, which opened the Venice Festival in 1971, was released in 1972 with screenplay by Andrew Sinclair and starring Richard Burton and Peter O'Toole.

On the 9th of November 1953, a few days after his thirty-ninth birthday, Dylan Thomas died in New York. At the time of his death a new poem was still unfinished, and the collaboration with Stravinsky, planned for the end of the year, had not even begun. The survival of *Under Milk Wood* is a remarkable piece of good fortune, for it was not completed until Thomas came within a month of his death, though he had worked intermittently on the play for nearly ten years. There was no time for any final revision of the text by the poet himself, but we are justified in regarding what he has left as a complete work.

The publication of Thomas's *Collected Poems* in 1952 marked the end of one period of his literary development; after this, according to his own words, he intended to turn from the strictly personal kind of poetry to a more public form of expression, and to large-scale dramatic works in particular, where there would be scope for all his versatility, for his gifts of humour and characterization as well as his genius for poetry. It is fortunate that at least one of these projected works has been preserved for us.

*Under Milk Wood, a Play for Voices* grew by a slow and natural process, and the story of that growth, known only to a few friends of the poet, is most interesting. Thomas liked small towns by the sea best, and small Welsh towns by the sea best of all. Before the war he lived for many years in Laugharne, and during the war for a time in New Quay; there is no doubt that he absorbed the spirit of these places and, through imagination and insight, the spirit of all other places like them. When, more than ten years ago, a short talk was commissioned by the B.B.C., the description of a small Welsh seaside town was a natural choice of subject. *Quite Early One Morning*, short as it is, and written so many years ago, is closely related to *Under Milk Wood*. There is the same sequence of time, though limited to the morning hours and in winter, not spring; we hear the dreams of the sleeping town and see the sleepers getting up and going about their business. Captain Tiny Evans and the Rev. Thomas Evans are pygmies beside the blind sea-captain and the reverend bard of Llareggub, but Miss Hughes 'The Cosy' recalls

Myfanwy Price, Manchester House stands ready for Mog Edwards, and the husbands of Mrs Ogmore-Pritchard are already at their tasks: 'Dust the china, feed the canary, sweep the drawing-room floor; and before you let the sun in, mind he wipes his shoes.'

The success of this broadcast talk suggested to Thomas a more extended work against the same kind of background. At first he was unable to decide upon the form of the work, and there was much discussion with friends about a stage play, a comedy in verse, and a radio play with a blind man as narrator and central character. The blind man, a natural bridge between eye and ear for the radio listener, survives in *Under Milk Wood*, with the difference that Captain Cat is made to share his central position with two anonymous narrators. But the simple time sequence of *Quite Early One Morning*, which resembles the pattern of *Under Milk Wood* so closely, at first appeared inadequate; some kind of plot seemed to be necessary. Thomas thought he had found the theme he wanted in the contrast between the mythical town and the surrounding world, the conflict between the eccentrics, strong in their individuality and freedom, and the sane ones who sacrifice everything to some notion of conformity. The whole population cannot very well be accommodated inside the walls of a lunatic asylum; so the sane world decrees that the town itself shall be declared an 'insane area', with all traffic and goods diverted from it. Captain Cat, spokesman of the indignant citizens, insists that the sanity of the town should be put on trial in the town hall with every legal formality; he will be Counsel for the Defence and the citizens themselves will be witnesses. The trial takes place, but it comes to a surprising end. The final speech for the Prosecution consists of a full and minute description of the ideally sane town; as soon as they hear this, the people withdraw their defence and beg to be cordoned off from the sane world as soon as possible.

Once more settled in his house overlooking Laugharne Estuary, Thomas began working according to the plan of *The Town Was Mad*, as he called it, and brought the action up to the delivery of letters by Willy Nilly the postman; but by that time he had changed his mind, and there was no letter for Captain Cat about the sanity or the insanity of the town. When this first part of *Under Milk Wood*, with the provisional title *Llareggub, a Piece for Radio Perhaps*, appeared for the first time in *Botteghe Oscure*,[1] Thomas had returned to the plan of *Quite Early One Morning*; his intention was to limit the picture to the town itself, with hardly a suggestion of a world beyond the town, and to extend the time sequence to form a complete cycle.

[1] *Quaderno IX*, edited by Marguerite Caetani (Rome, 1952).

Before Thomas's third visit to the U.S.A. in 1953, the title *Under Milk Wood, a Play for Voices* was decided upon, the first part, *Llareggub*, was revised, and the work had been extended to the end of Polly Garter's song, where it first appears. In this form the play was read at the Kaufmann Auditorium of the Young Men's Hebrew Association on the 15th and the 29th of May; the poet himself read the parts of the First Voice and the Rev. Eli Jenkins.

As soon as Thomas returned to Britain the B.B.C. urged him to complete the work without further delay, and, by omitting some projected ballads and unfinished material for the closing section, he was able to supply a finished version at the end of October. The first broadcast of the whole work, produced by Douglas Cleverdon with a distinguished all Welsh cast, was given on the 25th of January 1954, with a repetition two days later.

In case *Under Milk Wood* falls into the hands of a Welsh philologist, it must be made clear that the language used is Anglo-Welsh. Dylan Thomas spoke no Welsh, and the reader must imitate his inconsistency if he wishes to hear the words as they were pronounced by the poet himself. A note on pronunciation will be found following the Second Preface.

*January 1954*                                         DANIEL JONES


## Second Preface

Twenty years have passed since I wrote the first Preface to *Under Milk Wood*, and in the course of that time the play has proved its enduring quality. It has been read privately, read publicly, staged and translated into many languages. In my view, the fame of Dylan Thomas will rest ultimately on a handful of poems; but, in the meantime, *Under Milk Wood* is surely his most widely known composition. Many who have read the play or heard it read many times are afraid to face any other work of Dylan Thomas, except perhaps the apparently straightforward stories of *Portrait of the Artist as a Young Dog* and one or two radio scripts.

This fear is not altogether unreasonable. Thomas's work inhabits two different worlds: the private, introspective world of his most concentrated and meticulously constructed poems, and the public, extrovert world of his broadly humorous and highly coloured 'prose'. *Under Milk Wood* belongs in the main to the second world, in which Thomas was guided to some extent by professional opportunism, and purposely aimed at immediate effect and accessibility. This does not lessen the quality of the play. Thomas would have failed in his professionalism if he had not recognized that in this medium, unlike the 'private' medium of a poem, the larger-than-life and the obvious-to-the-edge-of-vulgarity are not only forgivable, they are often highly effective in characterization, situation and language.

But to leave the subject of medium at this point would be misleading. *Under Milk Wood* is not simply a play: it is a play *for Voices*. The medium is intermediate between a play and a poem, allowing and calling for characteristics shared by both. Embedded in the broadest passages, the roughest prose, the listener or the reader-listener will find some fine poetry, for example, in the Captain Cat-Rosie Probert dialogues— incidentally, Thomas's own favourite parts of the play. Captain Cat and the narrators serve as eyes only in a certain sense; the play, whether heard in the mind or from a stage, is meant for the ear, which, unlike the eye, imposes no limits upon the imagination.

The success of *Under Milk Wood* in translation is significant. Verbal subtlety, word-play, the rhythm and the essence of the poetry, the strongly individual style of the 'prose'—if that is what we can call it—all these are lost in the process of translation. What is left? Humour, characterization, images, structure, the forward movement of the play (the word 'plot' can hardly be used), and robustness. If I had to choose one word to describe the quality that has ensured the survival of the play after the ordeal of translation, I would choose 'vitality'.

In my Preface of twenty years ago there is one paragraph which I feel I should modify in the light of subsequent knowledge and reflection. In the first paragraph, leaning a little heavily on editorial privilege, I imply that *Under Milk Wood* was completed; at the same time I mention the lack of final revision and express an opinion I still hold: 'we are justified in regarding what [Thomas] has left as a complete work'. Here it could be argued that this is a quibble on the words 'completed' and 'complete'. For us, *Under Milk Wood* is complete; for Dylan Thomas it was not completed. Quite apart from the work of revision, he intended to add a great deal to the evening sequence which, as it stands, is disproportionately short. He showed me some of this material. What I saw consisted chiefly of fragments of ballads to be sung by some of the main characters, for example, Bessie Bighead; the evening, like the morning, was to be 'all singing'. Even from these fragments, it was possible to guess how the ballads would turn out: the style would be 'mock sentimental eighteenth century', with some sexual innuendoes thrown in—like Mr Waldo's song, in fact. Llareggub's evening was evidently planned to be a celebration of maudlin drunkenness and ribaldry, and the date of events, from the vague 'recent present' of the opening of the play, was to slip back still further into the eighteenth century, the century in which Polly Garter always had lived.

The incompletness of *Under Milk Wood* caused textual difficulties, which were aggravated by Thomas's own alteration of words or phrases to suit American audiences. From a strictly scientific point of view only a variorum edition could unfold the whole story of deletions, substitutions, second thoughts, projected ideas, alternatives and so on. In my opinion, such an edition would be suitable only for the kind of reader who should never read *Under Milk Wood* at all; the play does not invite an academic approach. If this is true, textual responsibility in any edition of the play falls squarely on the shoulders of the editor, for good or for ill. My own aim has been to present a plain readable text, without fuss or distraction, and, above all, without additional reading or speaking directions, which serve only to limit the freedom of the reader's imagination. The text itself is already rich enough in suggestion and atmosphere.

Twenty years have taught me that something must also be said about the importance of the music in *Under Milk Wood*. To give one example: I have heard productions and public readings in which the Waldo Song was omitted. The disproportion of the evening sequence exists already; the omission of the song reduces that sequence to the proportion of a withered limb in the body of the play. Unfortunately, we are without the other ballads intended for the evening sequence, but at least we have the Waldo Song. Another point I would like to make concerns the casting of Polly Garter and Waldo. Obviously, these two characters, one of whom has almost nothing to say, should not be tone-deaf. On the other hand, they should not be professional singers. There is no music in *Under Milk Wood* meant to be performed with accuracy and polish; it should be sung as it would have been sung in Llareggub. In the finest public reading of *Under Milk Wood* I have ever heard—it was presented by players with real (not assumed) *South*-Walian accents—Waldo gave a rough, inaccurate, free interpretation of his song, and the whole cast joined in the refrain wildly, with abandon. The aim of this passage in the play had been achieved: here was the real pub atmosphere, after too-much-to-drink, and the sense of a time passed in carousing and singing was satisfied.

One last word about a word. At the time of first publication I was obliged against my will to change the name Llareggub to Llaregyb. In this edition I am glad to have the opportunity to see that the correct spelling is restored.

*August 1974*                                                    DANIEL JONES

# Notes on Pronunciation

[Page 11] *Rhiannon:* strongly aspirated *r*, and accent on the second syllable. *Llareggub:* a voiceless *l* produced from the side of the mouth, accent on the second syllable, the third syllable rhyming with 'bib'.

[Page 12] *Dai:* as 'dye'.

[Page 14] *Dowlais:* accent on the first syllable, the second syllable rhyming with 'ice'. *Maesgwyn:* mice-gwin, accent on the second syllable. *Myfanwy:* accent on the second syllable, *f* as *v*, the first *y* an indeterminate sound, the second *y* as *ee*.

[Page 15] *Ach y fi:* the *ch* guttural, the *y* indeterminate, *f* as *v*, the whole pronounced as one word; an interjection expressing disgust.

[Page 18] *mwchins:* a compromise between the English 'mooching' and the Welsh dialect word 'mitching', playing truant.

[Page 23] *Eisteddfodau:* eye-steth-vod-eye, the *th* voiced, a strong accent on the third syllable. *Parchs:* the *ch* guttural; clergymen.

[Page 24] *Organ Morgan:* the *r*'s rolled, the *o*'s short. *Gippo:* gypsy.

[Page 25] *Dewi:* de-wee, the first syllable, which has the accent, is short.

[Page 26] *Moel yr Wyddfa:* moil-er-ooithva, the *th* voiced. *Carnedd:* the *dd* a voiced *th*, the *r* rolled, accent on the first syllable. *Penmaenmawr:* 'maen' rhymes with 'line', 'mawr' with 'hour'. *Sawdde:* southay, the *th* voiced. *Edw:* aid-oo. *Llyfnant:* *y* indeterminate, *f* as *v*. *Claerwen, Cleddau, Dulais:* clire-wen; cleth-eye, the *th* voiced; dill-ice. *Ogwr:* ogoorr, accent on the first syllable. *Cennen:* the *c* hard.

[Page 34] *Gerwain:* Gerr-wine, the *g* hard. *Ty:* as 'tee'.

[Page 36] *Gorslas:* gorse-lahss, with a strong accent on the second syllable.

[Page 41] *Twll:* ooll, the *oo* short, the *ll* as in 'Llareggub'.

[Page 48] *cawl:* as 'cowl'; a broth with leeks.

[Page 63] *fach:* an expression of endearment; *f* and *v*, and the *ch* guttural.

[10]

[*Silence*]

FIRST VOICE (*Very softly*)
To begin at the beginning:
It is spring, moonless night in the small town, starless and
bible-black, the cobblestreets silent and the hunched,
courters'-and-rabbits' wood limping invisible down to the
sloeblack, slow, black, crowblack, fishingboat-bobbing sea.
The houses are blind as moles (though moles see fine to-night
in the snouting, velvet dingles) or blind as Captain Cat there
in the muffled middle by the pump and the town clock, the
shops in mourning, the Welfare Hall in widows' weeds. And
all the people of the lulled and dumbfound town are sleeping
now.

   Hush, the babies are sleeping, the farmers, the fishers, the
tradesmen and pensioners, cobbler, school-teacher, postman
and publican, the undertaker and the fancy woman, drunkard,
dressmaker, preacher, policeman, the webfoot cocklewomen
and the tidy wives. Young girls lie bedded soft or glide in
their dreams, with rings and trousseaux, bridesmaided by
glow-worms down the aisles of the organplaying wood. The
boys are dreaming wicked or of the bucking ranches of the
night and the jollyrodgered sea. And the anthracite statues
of the horses sleep in the fields, and the cows in the byres,
and the dogs in the wetnosed yards; and the cats nap in the
slant corners or lope sly, streaking and needling, on the one
cloud of the roofs.

   You can hear the dew falling, and the hushed town
breathing. Only *your* eyes are unclosed to see the black and
folded town fast, and slow, asleep. And you alone can hear
the invisible starfall, the darkest-before-dawn minutely
dewgrazed stir of the black, dab-filled sea where the *Arethusa*,
the *Curlew* and the *Skylark*, *Zanzibar*, *Rhiannon*, the *Rover*, the
*Cormorant*, and the *Star of Wales* tilt and ride.

   Listen. It is night moving in the streets, the processional
salt slow musical wind in Coronation Street and Cockle Row,
it is the grass growing on Llareggub Hill, dewfall, starfall,
the sleep of birds in Milk Wood.

Listen. It is night in the chill, squat chapel, hymning in bonnet and brooch and bombazine black, butterfly choker and bootlace bow, coughing like nannygoats, sucking mintoes, fortywinking hallelujah; night in the four-ale, quiet as a domino; in Ocky Milkman's loft like a mouse with gloves; in Dai Bread's bakery flying like black flour. It is to-night in Donkey Street, trotting silent, with seaweed on its hooves, along the cockled cobbles, past curtained fernpot, text and trinket, harmonium, holy dresser, watercolours done by hand, china dog and rosy tin teacaddy. It is night neddying among the snuggeries of babies.

Look. It is night, dumbly, royally winding through the Coronation cherry trees; going through the graveyard of Bethesda with winds gloved and folded, and dew doffed; tumbling by the Sailors Arms.

Time passes. Listen. Time passes.

Come closer now.

Only you can hear the houses sleeping in the streets in the slow deep salt and silent black, bandaged night. Only you can see, in the blinded bedrooms, the coms. and petticoats over the chairs, the jugs and basins, the glasses of teeth, Thou Shalt Not on the wall, and the yellowing dickybird-watching pictures of the dead. Only you can hear and see, behind the eyes of the sleepers, the movements and countries and mazes and colours and dismays and rainbows and tunes and wishes and flight and fall and despairs and big seas of their dreams.

From where you are, you can hear their dreams.

Captain Cat, the retired blind sea-captain, asleep in his bunk in the seashelled, ship-in-bottled, shipshape best cabin of Schooner House dreams of

SECOND VOICE
never such seas as any that swamped the decks of his S.S. *Kidwelly* bellying over the bedclothes and jellyfish-slippery sucking him down salt deep into the Davy dark where the fish come biting out and nibble him down to his wishbone, and the long drowned nuzzle up to him.

FIRST DROWNED
Remember me, Captain?

CAPTAIN CAT
You're Dancing Williams!

FIRST DROWNED
I lost my step in Nantucket.

SECOND DROWNED
Do you see me, Captain? the white bone talking? I'm

Tom-Fred the donkeyman . . . we shared the same girl once . . . her name was Mrs Probert . . .

WOMAN'S VOICE
Rosie Probert, thirty three Duck Lane. Come on up, boys, I'm dead.

THIRD DROWNED
Hold me, Captain, I'm Jonah Jarvis, come to a bad end, very enjoyable.

FOURTH DROWNED
Alfred Pomeroy Jones, sea-lawyer, born in Mumbles, sung like a linnet, crowned you with a flagon, tattooed with mermaids, thirst like a dredger, died of blisters.

FIRST DROWNED
This skull at your earhole is

FIFTH DROWNED
Curly Bevan. Tell my auntie it was me that pawned the ormolu clock.

CAPTAIN CAT
Aye, aye, Curly.

SECOND DROWNED
Tell my missus no I never

THIRD DROWNED
I never done what she said I never.

FOURTH DROWNED
Yes they did.

FIFTH DROWNED
And who brings coconuts and shawls and parrots to *my* Gwen now?

FIRST DROWNED
How's it above?

SECOND DROWNED
Is there rum and laverbread?

THIRD DROWNED
Bosoms and robins?

FOURTH DROWNED
Concertinas?

FIFTH DROWNED
Ebenezer's bell?

FIRST DROWNED
Fighting and onions?

**SECOND DROWNED**
And sparrows and daisies?

**THIRD DROWNED**
Tiddlers in a jamjar?

**FOURTH DROWNED**
Buttermilk and whippets?

**FIFTH DROWNED**
Rock-a-bye baby?

**FIRST DROWNED**
Washing on the line?

**SECOND DROWNED**
And old girls in the snug?

**THIRD DROWNED**
How's the tenors in Dowlais?

**FOURTH DROWNED**
Who milks the cows in Maesgwyn?

**FIFTH DROWNED**
When she smiles, is there dimples?

**FIRST DROWNED**
What's the smell of parsley?

**CAPTAIN CAT**
Oh, my dead dears!

**FIRST VOICE**
From where you are you can hear in Cockle Row in the
spring, moonless night, Miss Price, dressmaker and
sweetshop-keeper, dream of

**SECOND VOICE**
her lover, tall as the town clock tower, Samson-syrup-gold-
maned, whacking thighed and piping hot, thunderbolt-bass'd
and barnacle-breasted, flailing up the cockles with his eyes
like blowlamps and scooping low over her lonely loving
hotwaterbottled body.

**MR EDWARDS**
Myfanwy Price!

**MISS PRICE**
Mr Mog Edwards!

**MR EDWARDS**
I am a draper mad with love. I love you more than all the
flannelette and calico, candlewick, dimity, crash and merino,
tussore, cretonne, crepon, muslin, poplin, ticking and twill
in the whole Cloth Hall of the world. I have come to take

you away to my Emporium on the hill, where the change hums on wires. Throw away your little bedsocks and your Welsh wool knitted jacket, I will warm the sheets like an electric toaster, I will lie by your side like the Sunday roast.

MISS PRICE
I will knit you a wallet of forget-me-not blue, for the money to be comfy. I will warm your heart by the fire so that you can slip it in under your vest when the shop is closed.

MR EDWARDS
Myfanwy, Myfanwy, before the mice gnaw at your bottom drawer will you say

MISS PRICE
Yes, Mog, yes, Mog, yes, yes, yes.

MR EDWARDS
And all the bells of the tills of the town shall ring for our wedding.                        [*Noise of money-tills and chapel bells*

FIRST VOICE
Come now, drift up the dark, come up the drifting sea-dark street now in the dark night seesawing like the sea, to the bible-black airless attic over Jack Black the cobbler's shop where alone and savagely Jack Black sleeps in a nightshirt tied to his ankles with elastic and dreams of

SECOND VOICE
chasing the naughty couples down the grassgreen gooseberried double bed of the wood, flogging the tosspots in the spit-and-sawdust, driving out the bare bold girls from the sixpenny hops of his nightmares.

JACK BLACK (*Loudly*)
Ach y fi!
Ach y fi!

FIRST VOICE
Evans the Death, the undertaker,

SECOND VOICE
laughs high and aloud in his sleep and curls up his toes as he sees, upon waking fifty years ago, snow lie deep on the goosefield behind the sleeping house; and he runs out into the field where his mother is making welsh-cakes in the snow, and steals a fistful of snowflakes and currants and climbs back to bed to eat them cold and sweet under the warm, white clothes while his mother dances in the snow kitchen crying out for her lost currants.

FIRST VOICE
And in the little pink-eyed cottage next to the undertaker's, lie, alone, the seventeen snoring gentle stone of Mister Waldo, rabbitcatcher, barber, herbalist, catdoctor, quack, his fat pink hands, palms up, over the edge of the patchwork quilt, his black boots neat and tidy in the washing-basin, his bowler on a nail above the bed, a milk stout and a slice of cold bread pudding under the pillow; and, dripping in the dark, he dreams of

MOTHER
This little piggy went to market
This little piggy stayed at home
This little piggy had roast beef
This little piggy had none
And this little piggy went

LITTLE BOY
wee wee wee wee wee

MOTHER
all the way home to

WIFE (*Screaming*)
Waldo! Wal-do!

MR WALDO
Yes, Blodwen love?

WIFE
Oh, what'll the neighbours say, what'll the neighbours . . .

FIRST NEIGHBOUR
Poor Mrs Waldo

SECOND NEIGHBOUR
What she puts up with

FIRST NEIGHBOUR
Never should of married

SECOND NEIGHBOUR
If she didn't had to

FIRST NEIGHBOUR
Same as her mother

SECOND NEIGHBOUR
There's a husband for you

FIRST NEIGHBOUR
Bad as his father

SECOND NEIGHBOUR
And you know where he ended

FIRST NEIGHBOUR
  Up in the asylum

SECOND NEIGHBOUR
  Crying for his ma

FIRST NEIGHBOUR
  Every Saturday

SECOND NEIGHBOUR
  He hasn't got a leg

FIRST NEIGHBOUR
  And carrying on

SECOND NEIGHBOUR
  With that Mrs Beattie Morris

FIRST NEIGHBOUR
  Up in the quarry

SECOND NEIGHBOUR
  And seen her baby

FIRST NEIGHBOUR
  It's got his nose

SECOND NEIGHBOUR
  Oh it makes my heart bleed

FIRST NEIGHBOUR
  What he'll do for drink

SECOND NEIGHBOUR
  He sold the pianola

FIRST NEIGHBOUR
  And her sewing machine

SECOND NEIGHBOUR
  Falling in the gutter

FIRST NEIGHBOUR
  Talking to the lamp-post

SECOND NEIGHBOUR
  Using language

FIRST NEIGHBOUR
  Singing in the w

SECOND NEIGHBOUR
  Poor Mrs Waldo

WIFE (*Tearfully*)
  . . . Oh, Waldo, Waldo!

MR WALDO
  Hush, love, hush. I'm *widower* Waldo now.

MOTHER (*Screaming*)
Waldo, Wal-do!

LITTLE BOY
Yes, our mum?

MOTHER
Oh, what'll the neighbours say, what'll the neighbours . . .

THIRD NEIGHBOUR
Black as a chimbley

FOURTH NEIGHBOUR
Ringing doorbells

THIRD NEIGHBOUR
Breaking windows

FOURTH NEIGHBOUR
Making mudpies

THIRD NEIGHBOUR
Stealing currants

FOURTH NEIGHBOUR
Chalking words

THIRD NEIGHBOUR
Saw him in the bushes

FOURTH NEIGHBOUR
Playing mwchins

THIRD NEIGHBOUR
Send him to bed without any supper

FOURTH NEIGHBOUR
Give him sennapods and lock him in the dark

THIRD NEIGHBOUR
Off to the reformatory

FOURTH NEIGHBOUR
Off to the reformatory

TOGETHER
Learn him with a slipper on his b.t.m.

ANOTHER MOTHER (*Screaming*)
Waldo, Wal-do! what you doing with our Matti?

LITTLE BOY
Give us a kiss, Matti Richards.

LITTLE GIRL
Give us a penny then.

MR WALDO
I only got a halfpenny.

[18]

**FIRST WOMAN**
Lips is a penny.

**PREACHER**
Will you take this woman Matti Richards

**SECOND WOMAN**
Dulcie Prothero

**THIRD WOMAN**
Effie Bevan

**FOURTH WOMAN**
Lil the Gluepot

**FIFTH WOMAN**
Mrs Flusher

**WIFE**
Blodwen Bowen

**PREACHER**
To be your awful wedded wife

**LITTLE BOY** (*Screaming*)
No, no, no!

**FIRST VOICE**
Now, in her iceberg-white, holily laundered crinoline
nightgown, under virtuous polar sheets, in her spruced and
scoured dust-defying bedroom in trig and trim Bay View, a
house for paying guests, at the top of the town, Mrs
Ogmore-Pritchard widow, twice, of Mr Ogmore, linoleum,
retired, and Mr Pritchard, failed bookmaker, who maddened
by besoming, swabbing and scrubbing, the voice of the
vacuum-cleaner and the fume of polish, ironically swallowed
disinfectant, fidgets in her rinsed sleep, wakes in a dream, and
nudges in the ribs dead Mr Ogmore, dead Mr Pritchard,
ghostly on either side.

**MRS OGMORE-PRITCHARD**
Mr Ogmore!
Mr Pritchard!
It is time to inhale your balsam.

**MR OGMORE**
Oh, Mrs Ogmore!

**MR PRITCHARD**
Oh, Mrs Pritchard!

**MRS OGMORE-PRITCHARD**
Soon it will be time to get up.
Tell me your tasks, in order.

MR OGMORE
   I must put my pyjamas in the drawer marked pyjamas.

MR PRITCHARD
   I must take my cold bath which is good for me.

MR OGMORE
   I must wear my flannel band to ward off sciatica.

MR PRITCHARD
   I must dress behind the curtain and put on my apron.

MR OGMORE
   I must blow my nose.

MRS OGMORE-PRITCHARD
   In the garden, if you please.

MR OGMORE
   In a piece of tissue-paper which I afterwards burn.

MR PRITCHARD
   I must take my salts which are nature's friend.

MR OGMORE
   I must boil the drinking water because of germs.

MR PRITCHARD
   I must make my herb tea which is free from tannin.

MR OGMORE
   And have a charcoal biscuit which is good for me.

MR PRITCHARD
   I may smoke one pipe of asthma mixture.

MRS OGMORE-PRITCHARD
   In the woodshed, if you please.

MR PRITCHARD
   And dust the parlour and spray the canary.

MR OGMORE
   I must put on rubber gloves and search the peke for fleas.

MR PRITCHARD
   I must dust the blinds and then I must raise them.

MRS OGMORE-PRITCHARD
   And before you let the sun in, mind it wipes its shoes.

FIRST VOICE
   In Butcher Beynon's, Gossamer Beynon, daughter,
   schoolteacher, dreaming deep, daintily ferrets under a
   fluttering hummock of chicken's feathers in a slaughterhouse
   that has chintz curtains and a three-pieced suite, and finds,
   with no surprise, a small rough ready man with a bushy tail
   winking in a paper carrier.

[20]

**GOSSAMER BEYNON**
At last, my love,

**FIRST VOICE**
sighs Gossamer Beynon. And the bushy tail wags rude and ginger.

**ORGAN MORGAN**
Help,

**SECOND VOICE**
cries Organ Morgan, the organist, in his dream,

**ORGAN MORGAN**
There is perturbation and music in Coronation Street! All the spouses are honking like geese and the babies singing opera. P.C. Attila Rees has got his truncheon out and is playing cadenzas by the pump, the cows from Sunday Meadow ring like reindeer, and on the roof of Handel Villa see the Women's Welfare hoofing, bloomered, in the moon.

**FIRST VOICE**
At the sea-end of town, Mr and Mrs Floyd, the cocklers, are sleeping as quiet as death, side by wrinkled side, toothless, salt and brown, like two old kippers in a box.
   And high above, in Salt Lake Farm, Mr Utah Watkins counts, all night, the wife-faced sheep as they leap the fences on the hill, smiling and knitting and bleating just like Mrs Utah Watkins.

**UTAH WATKINS** (*Yawning*)
Thirty-four, thirty-five, thirty-six, forty-eight, eighty-nine . . .

**MRS UTAH WATKINS** (*Bleating*)
Knit one slip one
Knit two together
Pass the slipstitch over . . .

**FIRST VOICE**
Ocky Milkman, drowned asleep in Cockle Street, is emptying his churns into the Dewi River,

**OCKY MILKMAN** (*Whispering*)
regardless of expense,

**FIRST VOICE**
and weeping like a funeral.

**SECOND VOICE**
Cherry Owen, next door, lifts a tankard to his lips but nothing flows out of it. He shakes the tankard. It turns into a fish. He drinks the fish.

**FIRST VOICE**

P.C. Attila Rees lumps out of bed, dead to the dark and still foghorning, and drags out his helmet from under the bed; but deep in the backyard lock-up of his sleep a mean voice murmurs.

**A VOICE** (*Murmuring*)

You'll be sorry for this in the morning,

**FIRST VOICE**

and he heave-ho's back to bed. His helmet swashes in the dark.

**SECOND VOICE**

Willy Nilly, postman, asleep up street, walks fourteen miles to deliver the post as he does every day of the night, and rat-a-tats hard and sharp on Mrs Willy Nilly.

**MRS WILLY NILLY**

Don't spank me, please, teacher,

**SECOND VOICE**

whimpers his wife at his side, but every night of her married life she has been late for school.

**FIRST VOICE**

Sinbad Sailors, over the taproom of the Sailors Arms, hugs his damp pillow whose secret name is Gossamer Beynon.
A mogul catches Lily Smalls in the wash-house.

**LILY SMALLS**

Ooh, you old mogul!

**SECOND VOICE**

Mrs Rose Cottage's eldest, Mae, peels off her pink-and-white skin in a furnace in a tower in a cave in a waterfall in a wood and waits there raw as an onion for Mister Right to leap up the burning tall hollow splashes of leaves like a brilliantined trout.

**MAE ROSE COTTAGE** (*Very close and softly*, *drawing out the words*)

Call me Dolores
Like they do in the stories.

**FIRST VOICE**

Alone until she dies, Bessie Bighead, hired help, born in the workhouse, smelling of the cowshed, snores bass and gruff on a couch of straw in a loft in Salt Lake Farm and picks a posy of daisies in Sunday Meadow to put on the grave of Gomer Owen who kissed her once by the pig-sty when she wasn't looking and never kissed her again although she was looking all the time.

And the Inspectors of Cruelty fly down into Mrs Butcher
Beynon's dream to persecute Mr Benyon for selling

BUTCHER BEYNON
owlmeat, dogs' eyes, manchop.

SECOND VOICE
Mr Beynon, in butcher's bloodied apron, spring-heels down
Coronation Street, a finger, not his own, in his mouth.
Straightfaced in his cunning sleep he pulls the legs of his
dreams and

BUTCHER BEYNON
hunting on pigback shoots down the wild giblets.

ORGAN MORGAN (*High and softly*)
Help!

GOSSAMER BEYNON (*Softly*)
My foxy darling.

FIRST VOICE
Now behind the eyes and secrets of the dreamers in the
streets rocked to sleep by the sea, see the

SECOND VOICE
titbits and topsyturvies, bobs and buttontops, bags and bones,
ash and rind and dandruff and nailparings, saliva and
snowflakes and moulted feathers of dreams, the wrecks and
sprats and shells and fishbones, whalejuice and moonshine
and small salt fry dished up by the hidden sea.

FIRST VOICE
The owls are hunting. Look, over Bethesda gravestones one
hoots and swoops and catches a mouse by Hannah Rees,
Beloved Wife. And in Coronation Street, which you alone
can see it is so dark under the chapel in the skies, the
Reverend Eli Jenkins, poet, preacher, turns in his deep
towards-dawn sleep and dreams of

REV. ELI JENKINS
Eisteddfodau.

SECOND VOICE
He intricately rhymes, to the music of crwth and pibgorn, all
night long in his druid's seedy nightie in a beer-tent black
with parchs.

FIRST VOICE
Mr Pugh, schoolmaster, fathoms asleep, pretends to be
sleeping, spies foxy round the droop of his nightcap and
pssst! whistles up

MR PUGH
Murder.

FIRST VOICE
   Mrs Organ Morgan, groceress, coiled grey like a dormouse,
   her paws to her ears, conjures

MRS ORGAN MORGAN
   Silence.

SECOND VOICE
   She sleeps very dulcet in a cove of wool, and trumpeting
   Organ Morgan at her side snores no louder than a spider.

FIRST VOICE
   Mary Ann Sailors dreams of

MARY ANN SAILORS
   The Garden of Eden.

FIRST VOICE
   She comes in her smock-frock and clogs

MARY ANN SAILORS
   away from the cool scrubbed cobbled kitchen with the
   Sunday-school pictures on the whitewashed wall and the
   farmers' almanac hung above the settle and the sides of bacon
   on the ceiling hooks, and goes down the cockleshelled paths
   of that applepie kitchen garden, ducking under the gippo's
   clothespegs, catching her apron on the blackcurrant bushes,
   past beanrows and onion-bed and tomatoes ripening on the
   wall towards the old man playing the harmonium in the
   orchard, and sits down on the grass at his side and shells the
   green peas that grow up through the lap of her frock that
   brushes the dew.

FIRST VOICE
   In Donkey Street, so furred with sleep, Dai Bread, Polly
   Garter, Nogood Boyo, and Lord Cut-Glass sigh before the
   dawn that is about to be and dream of

DAI BREAD
   Harems.

POLLY GARTER
   Babies.

NOGOOD BOYO
   Nothing.

LORD CUT-GLASS
   Tick tock tick tock tick tock tick tock.

FIRST VOICE
   Time passes. Listen. Time passes. An owl flies home past
   Bethesda, to a chapel in an oak. And the dawn inches up.
                    [*One distant bell-note, faintly reverberating*

FIRST VOICE

Stand on this hill. This is Llareggub Hill, old as the hills, high, cool, and green, and from this small circle of stones, made not by druids but by Mrs Beynon's Billy, you can see all the town below you sleeping in the first of the dawn.

You can hear the love-sick woodpigeons mooning in bed. A dog barks in his sleep, farmyards away. The town ripples like a lake in the waking haze.

VOICE OF A GUIDE-BOOK

Less than five hundred souls inhabit the three quaint streets and the few narrow by-lanes and scattered farmsteads that constitute this small, decaying watering-place which may, indeed, be called a 'backwater of life' without disrespect to its natives who possess, to this day, a salty individuality of their own. The main street, Coronation Street, consists, for the most part, of humble, two-storied houses many of which attempt to achieve some measure of gaiety by prinking themselves out in crude colours and by the liberal use of pinkwash, though there are remaining a few eighteenth-century houses of more pretension, if, on the whole, in a sad state of disrepair. Though there is little to attract the hillclimber, the healthseeker, the sportsman, or the weekending motorist, the contemplative may, if sufficiently attracted to spare it some leisurely hours, find, in its cobbled streets and its little fishing harbour, in its several curious customs, and in the conversation of its local 'characters', some of that picturesque sense of the past so frequently lacking in towns and villages which have kept more abreast of the times. The River Dewi is said to abound in trout, but is much poached. The one place of worship, with its neglected graveyard, is of no architectural interest.

[*A cock crows*

FIRST VOICE

The principality of the sky lightens now, over our green hill, into spring morning larked and crowed and belling.

[*Slow bell notes*

FIRST VOICE

Who pulls the townhall bellrope but blind Captain Cat? One by one, the sleepers are rung out of sleep this one morning as every morning. And soon you shall see the chimneys' slow upflying snow as Captain Cat, in sailor's cap and seaboots, announces to-day with his loud get-out-of-bed bell.

SECOND VOICE

The Reverend Eli Jenkins, in Bethesda House, gropes out of bed into his preacher's black, combs back his bard's white hair, forgets to wash, pads barefoot downstairs, opens the

[25]

front door, stands in the doorway and, looking out at the day and up at the eternal hill, and hearing the sea break and the gab of birds, remembers his own verses and tells them softly to empty Coronation Street that is rising and raising its blinds.

REV. ELI JENKINS

Dear Gwalia! I know there are
Towns lovelier than ours,
And fairer hills and loftier far,
And groves more full of flowers,

And boskier woods more blithe with spring
And bright with birds' adorning,
And sweeter bards than I to sing
Their praise this beauteous morning.

By Cader Idris, tempest-torn,
Or Moel yr Wyddfa's glory,
Carnedd Llewelyn beauty born,
Plinlimmon old in story,

By mountains where King Arthur dreams,
By Penmaenmawr defiant,
Llareggub Hill a molehill seems,
A pygmy to a giant.

By Sawdde, Senny, Dovey, Dee,
Edw, Eden, Aled, all,
Taff and Towy broad and free,
Llyfnant with its waterfall,

Claerwen, Cleddau, Dulais, Daw,
Ely, Gwili, Ogwr, Nedd,
Small is our River Dewi, Lord,
A baby on a rushy bed.

By Carreg Cennen, King of time,
Our Heron Head is only
A bit of stone with seaweed spread
Where gulls come to be lonely.

A tiny dingle is Milk Wood
By Golden Grove 'neath Grongar,
But let me choose and oh! I should
Love all my life and longer

To stroll among our trees and stray
In Goosegog Lane, on Donkey Down,
And hear the Dewi sing all day,
And never, never leave the town.

   The Reverend Jenkins closes the front door. His morning
   service is over.                        [*Slow bell notes*

FIRST VOICE
   Now, woken at last by the out-of-bed-sleepy-head-Polly-put-
   the-kettle-on townhall bell, Lily Smalls, Mrs Beynon's
   treasure, comes downstairs from a dream of royalty who all
   night long went larking with her full of sauce in the Milk
   Wood dark, and puts the kettle on the primus ring in Mrs
   Beynon's kitchen, and looks at herself in Mr Beynon's
   shaving-glass over the sink, and sees:

LILY SMALLS
   Oh there's a face!
   Where you get that hair from?
   Got it from a old tom cat.
   Give it back then, love.
   Oh there's a perm!

   Where you get that nose from, Lily?
   Got it from my father, silly.
   You've got it on upside down!
   Oh there's a conk!

   Look at your complexion!
   Oh no, *you* look.
   Needs a bit of make-up.
   Needs a veil.
   Oh there's glamour!

   Where you get that smile, Lil?
   Never you mind, girl.
   Nobody loves you.
   That's what *you* think.

   Who is it loves you?
   Shan't tell.
   Come on, Lily.
   Cross your heart then?
   Cross my heart.

FIRST VOICE
   And very softly, her lips almost touching her reflection, she
   breathes the name and clouds the shaving-glass.

MRS BEYNON (*Loudly, from above*)
   Lily!

LILY SMALLS (*Loudly*)
   Yes, mum.

MRS BEYNON
   Where's my tea, girl?

LILY SMALLS
   (*Softly*) Where d'you think? In the cat-box?
   (*Loudly*) Coming up, mum.

FIRST VOICE
   Mr Pugh, in the School House opposite, takes up the
   morning tea to Mrs Pugh, and whispers on the stairs

MR PUGH
   Here's your arsenic, dear.
   And your weedkiller biscuit.
   I've throttled your parakeet.
   I've spat in the vases.
   I've put cheese in the mouseholes.
   Here's your . . .                              [*Door creaks open*
   . . . nice tea, dear.

MRS PUGH
   Too much sugar.

MR PUGH
   You haven't tasted it yet, dear.

MRS PUGH
   Too much milk, then. Has Mr Jenkins said his poetry?

MR PUGH
   Yes, dear.

MRS PUGH
   Then it's time to get up. Give me my glasses.
   No, not my *reading* glasses, I want to look *out*. I want to see.

SECOND VOICE
   Lily Smalls the treasure down on her red knees washing the
   front step.

MRS PUGH
   She's tucked her dress in her bloomers—oh, the baggage!

SECOND VOICE
   P.C. Attila Rees, ox-broad, barge-booted, stamping out of
   Handcuff House in a heavy beef-red huff, black-browed under
   his damp helmet . . .

MRS PUGH
   He's going to arrest Polly Garter, mark my words.

MR PUGH
   What for, dear?

MRS PUGH
   For having babies.

[28]

SECOND VOICE
    . . . and lumbering down towards the strand to see that the
    sea is still there.

FIRST VOICE
    Mary Ann Sailors, opening her bedroom window above the
    taproom and calling out to the heavens

MARY ANN SAILORS
    I'm eighty-five years three months and a day!

MRS PUGH
    I will say this for her, she never makes a mistake.

FIRST VOICE
    Organ Morgan at his bedroom window playing chords on
    the sill to the morning fishwife gulls who, heckling over
    Donkey Street, observe

DAI BREAD
    Me, Dai Bread, hurrying to the bakery, pushing in my shirt-
    tails, buttoning my waistcoat, ping goes a button, why can't
    they sew them, no time for breakfast, nothing for breakfast,
    there's wives for you.

MRS DAI BREAD ONE
    Me, Mrs Dai Bread One, capped and shawled and no old
    corset, nice to be comfy, nice to be nice, clogging on the
    cobbles to stir up a neighbour. Oh, Mrs Sarah, can you spare
    a loaf, love? Dai Bread forgot the bread. There's a lovely
    morning! How's your boils this morning? Isn't that good
    news now, it's a change to sit down. Ta, Mrs Sarah.

MRS DAI BREAD TWO
    Me, Mrs Dai Bread Two, gypsied to kill in a silky scarlet
    petticoat above my knees, dirty pretty knees, see my body
    through my petticoat brown as a berry, high-heel shoes with
    one heel missing, tortoiseshell comb in my bright black slinky
    hair, nothing else at all but a dab of scent, lolling gaudy at
    the doorway, tell your fortune in the tea-leaves, scowling at
    the sunshine, lighting up my pipe.

LORD CUT-GLASS
    Me, Lord Cut-Glass, in an old frock-coat belonged to Eli
    Jenkins and a pair of postman's trousers from Bethesda
    Jumble, running out of doors to empty slops—mind there,
    Rover!—and then running in again, tick tock.

NOGOOD BOYO
    Me, Nogood Boyo, up to no good in the wash-house.

MISS PRICE
    Me, Miss Price, in my pretty print housecoat, deft at the

clothesline, natty as a jenny-wren, then pit-pat back to my egg in its cosy, my crisp toast-fingers, my home-made plum and butterpat.

POLLY GARTER
Me, Polly Garter, under the washing line, giving the breast in the garden to my bonny new baby. Nothing grows in our garden, only washing. And babies. And where's their fathers live, my love? Over the hills and far away. You're looking up at me now. I know what you're thinking, you poor little milky creature. You're thinking, you're no better than you should be, Polly, and that's good enough for me. Oh, isn't life a terrible thing, thank God?

[*Single long high chord on strings*

FIRST VOICE
Now frying-pans spit, kettles and cats purr in the kitchen. The town smells of seaweed and breakfast all the way down from Bay View, where Mrs Ogmore-Pritchard, in smock and turban, big-besomed to engage the dust, picks at her starchless bread and sips lemon-rind tea, to Bottom Cottage, where Mr Waldo, in bowler and bib, gobbles his bubble-and-squeak and kippers and swigs from the saucebottle. Mary Ann Sailors

MARY ANN SAILORS
praises the Lord who made porridge.

FIRST VOICE
Mr Pugh

MR PUGH
remembers ground glass as he juggles his omelet.

FIRST VOICE
Mrs Pugh

MRS PUGH
nags the salt-cellar.

FIRST VOICE
Willy Nilly postman

WILLY NILLY
downs his last bucket of black brackish tea and rumbles out bandy to the clucking back where the hens twitch and grieve for their tea-soaked sops.

FIRST VOICE
Mrs Willy Nilly

MRS WILLY NILLY
full of tea to her double-chinned brim broods and bubbles

over her coven of kettles on the hissing hot range always
ready to steam open the mail.

FIRST VOICE
The Reverend Eli Jenkins

REV. ELI JENKINS
finds a rhyme and dips his pen in his cocoa.

FIRST VOICE
Lord Cut-Glass in his ticking kitchen

LORD CUT-GLASS
scampers from clock to clock, a bunch of clock-keys in one
hand, a fish-head in the other.

FIRST VOICE
Captain Cat in his galley

CAPTAIN CAT
blind and fine-fingered savours his sea-fry.

FIRST VOICE
Mr and Mrs Cherry Owen, in their Donkey Street room that
is bedroom, parlour, kitchen, and scullery, sit down to last
night's supper of onions boiled in their overcoats and broth
of spuds and baconrind and leeks and bones.

MRS CHERRY OWEN
See that smudge on the wall by the picture of Auntie
Blossom? That's where you threw the sago.
                              [*Cherry Owen laughs with delight*

MRS CHERRY OWEN
You only missed me by a inch.

CHERRY OWEN
I always miss Auntie Blossom too.

MRS CHERRY OWEN
Remember last night? In you reeled, my boy, as drunk as a
deacon with a big wet bucket and a fish-frail full of stout
and you looked at me and you said, 'God has come home!'
you said, and then over the bucket you went, sprawling and
bawling, and the floor was all flagons and eels.

CHERRY OWEN
Was I wounded?

MRS CHERRY OWEN
And then you took off your trousers and you said, 'Does
anybody want a fight!' Oh, you old baboon.

CHERRY OWEN
   Give me a kiss.

MRS CHERRY OWEN
   And then you sang 'Bread of Heaven', tenor and bass.

CHERRY OWEN
   I *always* sing 'Bread of Heaven'.

MRS CHERRY OWEN
   And then you did a little dance on the table.

CHERRY OWEN
   I did?

MRS CHERRY OWEN
   Drop dead!

CHERRY OWEN
   And then what did I do?

MRS CHERRY OWEN
   Then you cried like a baby and said you were a poor drunk
   orphan with nowhere to go but the grave.

CHERRY OWEN
   And what did I do next, my dear?

MRS CHERRY OWEN
   Then you danced on the table all over again and said you
   were King Solomon Owen and I was your Mrs Sheba.

CHERRY OWEN (*Softly*)
   And then?

MRS CHERRY OWEN
   And then I got you into bed and you snored all night like a
   brewery.          [*Mr and Mrs Cherry Owen laugh delightedly together*

FIRST VOICE
   From Beynon Butchers in Coronation Street, the smell of
   fried liver sidles out with onions on its breath. And listen!
   In the dark breakfast-room behind the shop, Mr and Mrs
   Beynon, waited upon by their treasure, enjoy, between bites,
   their everymorning hullabaloo, and Mrs Beynon slips the
   gristly bits under the tasselled tablecloth to her fat cat.
                                                    [*Cat purrs*

MRS BEYNON
   She likes the liver, Ben.

MR BEYNON
   She ought to do, Bess. It's her brother's.

MRS BEYNON (*Screaming*)
   Oh, d'you hear that, Lily?

LILY SMALLS
  Yes, mum.

MRS BEYNON
  We're eating pusscat.

LILY SMALLS
  Yes, mum.

MRS BEYNON
  Oh, you cat-butcher!

MR BEYNON
  It was doctored, mind.

MRS BEYNON (*Hysterical*)
  What's that got to do with it?

MR BEYNON
  Yesterday we had mole.

MRS BEYNON
  Oh, Lily, Lily!

MR BEYNON
  Monday, otter. Tuesday, shrews.        [*Mrs Beynon screams*

LILY SMALLS
  Go on, Mrs Beynon. He's the biggest liar in town.

MRS BEYNON
  Don't you dare say that about Mr Beynon.

LILY SMALLS
  Everybody knows it, mum.

MRS BEYNON
  Mr Beynon never tells a lie. Do you, Ben?

MR BEYNON
  No, Bess, And now I am going out after the corgies, with
  my little cleaver.

MRS BEYNON
  Oh, Lily, Lily!

FIRST VOICE
  Up the street, in the Sailors Arms, Sinbad Sailors, grandson
  of Mary Ann Sailors, draws a pint in the sunlit bar. The
  ship's clock in the bar says half past eleven. Half past eleven
  is opening time. The hands of the clock have stayed still at
  half past eleven for fifty years. It is always opening time in
  the Sailors Arms.

SINBAD
  Here's to me, Sinbad.

FIRST VOICE
  All over the town, babies and old men are cleaned and put
  into their broken prams and wheeled on to the sunlit cockled
  cobbles or out into the backyards under the dancing
  underclothes, and left. A baby cries.

OLD MAN
  I want my pipe and he wants his bottle.　　　[*School bell rings*

FIRST VOICE
  Noses are wiped, heads picked, hair combed, paws scrubbed,
  ears boxed, and the children shrilled off to school.

SECOND VOICE
  Fishermen grumble to their nets. Nogood Boyo goes out in
  the dinghy *Zanzibar*, ships the oars, drifts slowly in the dab-
  filled bay, and, lying on his back in the unbaled water, among
  crabs' legs and tangled lines, looks up at the spring sky.

NOGOOD BOYO (*Softly, lazily*)
  I don't know who's up there and I don't care.

FIRST VOICE
  He turns his head and looks up at Llareggub Hill, and sees,
  among green lathered trees, the white houses of the strewn
  away farms, where farmboys whistle, dogs shout, cows low,
  but all too far away for him, or you, to hear. And in the
  town, the shops squeak open. Mr Edwards, in butterfly-collar
  and straw-hat at the doorway of Manchester House, measures
  with his eye the dawdlers-by for striped flannel shirts and
  shrouds and flowery blouses, and bellows to himself in the
  darkness behind his eye

MR EDWARDS (*Whispers*)
  I love Miss Price.

FIRST VOICE
  Syrup is sold in the post-office. A car drives to market, full
  of fowls and a farmer. Milk-churns stand at Coronation
  Corner like short silver policemen. And, sitting at the open
  window of Schooner House, blind Captain Cat hears all the
  morning of the town.
　　　　　　　[*School bell in background. Children's voices. The
　　　　　　　　　noise of children's feet on the cobbles*

CAPTAIN CAT (*Softly, to himself*)
  Maggie Richards, Ricky Rhys, Tommy Powell, our Sal, little
  Gerwain, Billy Swansea with the dog's voice, one of Mr
  Waldo's, nasty Humphrey, Jackie with the sniff. . . . Where's
  Dicky's Albie? and the boys from Ty-pant? Perhaps they got
  the rash again.　　　　　　　[*A sudden cry among the children's voices*

[34]

CAPTAIN CAT
Somebody's hit Maggie Richards. Two to one it's Billy
Swansea. Never trust a boy who barks.
[*A burst of yelping crying*
Right again! It's Billy.

FIRST VOICE
And the children's voices cry away.
[*Postman's rat-a-tat on door, distant*

CAPTAIN CAT (*Softly, to himself*)
That's Willy Nilly knocking at Bay View. Rat-a-tat, very soft.
The knocker's got a kid glove on. Who's sent a letter to
Mrs Ogmore-Pritchard?
[*Rat-a-tat, distant again*

CAPTAIN CAT
Careful now, she swabs the front glassy. Every step's like a
bar of soap. Mind your size twelveses. That old Bessie would
beeswax the lawn to make the birds slip.

WILLY NILLY
Morning, Mrs Ogmore-Pritchard.

MRS OGMORE-PRITCHARD
Good morning, postman.

WILLY NILLY
Here's a letter for you with stamped and addressed envelope
enclosed, all the way from Builth Wells. A gentleman wants
to study birds and can he have accommodation for two weeks
and a bath vegetarian.

MRS OGMORE-PRITCHARD
No.

WILLY NILLY (*Persuasively*)
You wouldn't know he was in the house, Mrs Ogmore-
Pritchard. He'd be out in the mornings at the bang of dawn
with his bag of breadcrumbs and his little telescope . . .

MRS OGMORE-PRITCHARD
And come home at all hours covered with feathers. I don't
want persons in my nice clean rooms breathing all over the
chairs . . .

WILLY NILLY
Cross my heart, he won't breathe.

MRS OGMORE-PRITCHARD
. . . and putting their feet on my carpets and sneezing on my
china and sleeping in my sheets . . .

WILLY NILLY
    He only wants a *single* bed, Mrs Ogmore-Pritchard.

[*Door slams*

CAPTAIN CAT (*Softly*)
    And back she goes to the kitchen to polish the potatoes.

FIRST VOICE
    Captain Cat hears Willy Nilly's feet heavy on the distant
    cobbles.

CAPTAIN CAT
    One, two, three, four, five. . . . That's Mrs Rose Cottage.
    What's to-day? To-day she gets the letter from her sister in
    Gorslas. How's the twins' teeth?
        He's stopping at School House.

WILLY NILLY
    Morning, Mrs Pugh. Mrs Ogmore-Pritchard won't have a
    gentleman in from Builth Wells because he'll sleep in her
    sheets, Mrs Rose Cottage's sister in Gorslas's twins have got
    to have them out . . .

MRS PUGH
    Give me the parcel.

WILLY NILLY
    It's for *Mr* Pugh, Mrs Pugh.

MRS PUGH
    Never you mind. What's inside it?

WILLY NILLY
    A book called *Lives of the Great Poisoners*.

CAPTAIN CAT
    That's Manchester House.

WILLY NILLY
    Morning, Mr Edwards. Very small news. Mrs Ogmore-
    Pritchard won't have birds in the house, and Mr Pugh's
    bought a book now on how to do in Mrs Pugh.

MR EDWARDS
    Have you got a letter from *her*?

WILLY NILLY
    Miss Price loves you with all her heart. Smelling of lavender
    to-day. She's down to the last of the elderflower wine but
    the quince jam's bearing up and she's knitting roses on the
    doilies. Last week she sold three jars of boiled sweets, pound
    of humbugs, half a box of jellybabies and six coloured photos
    of Llareggub. Yours for ever. Then twenty-one X's.

MR EDWARDS
Oh, Willy Nilly, she's a ruby! Here's my letter. Put it into her hands now. [*Slow feet on cobbles, quicker feet approaching*

CAPTAIN CAT
Mr Waldo hurrying to the Sailors Arms. Pint of stout with a egg in it. [*Footsteps stop*
(*Softly*) There's a letter for him.

WILLY NILLY
It's another paternity summons, Mr Waldo.

FIRST VOICE
The quick footsteps hurry on along the cobbles and up three steps to the Sailors Arms.

MR WALDO (*Calling out*)
Quick, Sinbad. Pint of stout. And no egg in.

FIRST VOICE
People are moving now up and down the cobbled street.

CAPTAIN CAT
All the women are out this morning, in the sun. You can tell it's Spring. There goes Mrs Cherry, you can tell her by her trotters, off she trots new as a daisy. Who's that talking by the pump? Mrs Floyd and Boyo, talking flatfish. What can you talk about flatfish? That's Mrs Dai Bread One, waltzing up the street like a jelly, every time she shakes it's slap slap slap. Who's that? Mrs Butcher Beynon with her pet black cat, it follows her everywhere, miaow and all. There goes Mrs Twenty-Three, important, the sun gets up and goes down in her dewlap, when she shuts her eyes, it's night. High heels now, in the morning too, Mrs Rose Cottage's eldest Mae, seventeen and never been kissed ho ho, going young and milking under my window to the field with the nannygoats, she reminds me all the way. Can't hear what the women are gabbing round the pump. Same as ever. Who's having a baby, who blacked whose eye, seen Polly Garter giving her belly an airing, there should be a law, seen Mrs Beynon's new mauve jumper, it's her old grey jumper dyed, who's dead, who's dying, there's a lovely day, oh the cost of soapflakes! [*Organ music, distant*

CAPTAIN CAT
Organ Morgan's at it early. You can tell it's Spring.

FIRST VOICE
And he hears the noise of milk-cans.

CAPTAIN CAT
Ocky Milkman on his round. I will say this, his milk's as

fresh as the dew. Half dew it is. Snuffle on, Ocky, watering the town . . . Somebody's coming. Now the voices round the pump can see somebody coming. Hush, there's a hush! You can tell by the noise of the hush, it's Polly Garter. (*Louder*) Hullo, Polly, who's there?

POLLY GARTER (*Off*)
Me, love.

CAPTAIN CAT
*That's* Polly Garter. (*Softly*) Hullo, Polly my love, can you hear the dumb goose-hiss of the wives as they huddle and peck or flounce at a waddle away? Who cuddled you when? Which of their gandering hubbies moaned in Milk Wood for your naughty mothering arms and body like a wardrobe, love? Scrub the floors of the Welfare Hall for the Mothers' Union Social Dance, you're one mother won't wriggle her roly poly bum or pat her fat little buttery feet in that wedding-ringed holy to-night though the waltzing breadwinners snatched from the cosy smoke of the Sailors Arms will grizzle and mope.

[*A cock crows*

CAPTAIN CAT
Too late, cock, too late

SECOND VOICE
for the town's half over with its morning. The morning's busy as bees.

[*Organ music fades into silence*

FIRST VOICE
There's the clip clop of horses on the sunhoneyed cobbles of the humming streets, hammering of horse-shoes, gobble quack and cackle, tomtit twitter from the bird-ounced boughs, braying on Donkey Down. Bread is baking, pigs are grunting, chop goes the butcher, milk-churns bell, tills ring, sheep cough, dogs shout, saws sing. Oh, the Spring whinny and morning moo from the clog dancing farms, the gulls' gab and rabble on the boat-bobbing river and sea and the cockles bubbling in the sand, scamper of sanderlings, curlew cry, crow caw, pigeon coo, clock strike, bull bellow, and the ragged gabble of the beargarden school as the women scratch and babble in Mrs Organ Morgan's general shop where everything is sold: custard, buckets, henna, rat-traps, shrimp-nets, sugar, stamps, confetti, paraffin, hatchets, whistles.

FIRST WOMAN
Mrs Ogmore-Pritchard

SECOND WOMAN
la di da

FIRST WOMAN
  got a man in Builth Wells

THIRD WOMAN
  and he got a little telescope to look at birds

SECOND WOMAN
  Willy Nilly said

THIRD WOMAN
  Remember her first husband? He didn't need a telescope

FIRST WOMAN
  he looked at them undressing through the keyhole

THIRD WOMAN
  and he used to shout Tallyho

SECOND WOMAN
  but Mr Ogmore was a proper gentleman

FIRST WOMAN
  even though he hanged his collie.

THIRD WOMAN
  Seen Mrs Butcher Beynon?

SECOND WOMAN
  she said Butcher Beynon put dogs in the mincer

FIRST WOMAN
  go on, he's pulling her leg

THIRD WOMAN
  now don't you dare tell her that, there's a dear

SECOND WOMAN
  or she'll think he's trying to pull it off and eat it.

FOURTH WOMAN
  There's a nasty lot live here when you come to think.

FIRST WOMAN
  Look at that Nogood Boyo now

SECOND WOMAN
  too lazy to wipe his snout

THIRD WOMAN
  and going out fishing every day and all he ever brought back
  was a Mrs Samuels

FIRST WOMAN
  been in the water a week.

SECOND WOMAN
  And look at Ocky Milkman's wife that nobody's ever seen

[39]

FIRST WOMAN
  he keeps her in the cupboard with the empties

THIRD WOMAN
  and think of Dai Bread with two wives

SECOND WOMAN
  one for the daytime one for the night.

FOURTH WOMAN
  Men are brutes on the quiet.

THIRD WOMAN
  And how's Organ Morgan, Mrs Morgan?

FIRST WOMAN
  you look dead beat

SECOND WOMAN
  it's organ organ all the time with him

THIRD WOMAN
  up every night until midnight playing the organ.

MRS ORGAN MORGAN
  Oh, I'm a martyr to music.

FIRST VOICE
  Outside, the sun springs down on the rough and tumbling
  town. It runs through the hedges of Goosegog Lane, cuffing
  the birds to sing. Spring whips green down Cockle Row,
  and the shells ring out. Llareggub this snip of a morning is
  wildfruit and warm, the streets, fields, sands and waters
  springing in the young sun.

SECOND VOICE
  Evans the Death presses hard with black gloves on the coffin
  of his breast in case his heart jumps out.

EVANS THE DEATH (*Harshly*)
  Where's your dignity. Lie down.

SECOND VOICE
  Spring stirs Gossamer Beynon schoolmistress like a spoon.

GOSSAMER BEYNON (*Tearfully*)
  Oh, what can I do? I'll *never* be refined if I twitch.

SECOND VOICE
  Spring this strong morning foams in a flame in Jack Black
  as he cobbles a high-heeled shoe for Mrs Dai Bread Two the
  gypsy, but he hammers it sternly out.

JACK BLACK (*To a hammer rhythm*)
  There is *no leg* belonging to the foot that belongs to this shoe.

SECOND VOICE

The sun and the green breeze ship Captain Cat sea-memory again.

CAPTAIN CAT

No, *I'll* take the mulatto, by God, who's captain here? Parlez-vous jig jig, Madam?

SECOND VOICE

Mary Ann Sailors says very softly to herself as she looks out at Llareggub Hill from the bedroom where she was born

MARY ANN SAILORS (*Loudly*)

It is Spring in Llareggub in the sun in my old age, and this is the Chosen Land.

> [*A choir of children's voices suddenly cries out on one, high, glad, long, sighing note*

FIRST VOICE

And in Willy Nilly the Postman's dark and sizzling damp tea-coated misty pygmy kitchen where the spittingcat kettles throb and hop on the range, Mrs Willy Nilly steams open Mr Mog Edwards' letter to Miss Myfanwy Price and reads it aloud to Willy Nilly by the squint of the Spring sun through the one sealed window running with tears, while the drugged, bedraggled hens at the back door whimper and snivel for the lickerish bog-black tea.

MRS WILLY NILLY

From Manchester House, Llareggub. Sole Prop: Mr Mog Edwards (late of Twll), Linendraper, Haberdasher, Master Tailor, Costumier. For West End Negligee, Lingerie, Teagowns, Evening Dress, Trousseaux, Layettes. Also Ready to Wear for All Occasions. Economical Outfitting for Agricultural Employment Our Speciality, Wardrobes Bought. Among Our Satisfied Customers Ministers of Religion and J.P.'s. Fittings by Appointment. Advertising Weekly in the *Twll Bugle*. Beloved Myfanwy Price my Bride in Heaven,

MOG EDWARDS

I love you until Death do us part and then we shall be together for ever and ever. A new parcel of ribbons has come from Carmarthen to-day, all the colours in the rainbow. I wish I could tie a ribbon in your hair a white one but it cannot be. I dreamed last night you were all dripping wet and you sat on my lap as the Reverend Jenkins went down the street. I see you got a mermaid in your lap he said and he lifted his hat. He is a proper Christian. Not like Cherry Owen who said you should have thrown her back he said. Business is very poorly. Polly Garter bought two garters with roses but she never got stockings so what is the use I say. Mr Waldo tried to sell me a woman's nightie outsize he said he found it and we know where. I sold a packet of pins to Tom the Sailors to pick his teeth. If this goes on I shall be in the workhouse. My heart is in your bosom and yours is in mine. God be with you always Myfanwy Price and keep you lovely for me in His Heavenly Mansion. I must stop now and remain, Your Eternal, Mog Edwards.

MRS WILLY NILLY
And then a little message with a rubber stamp. Shop at Mog's!!!

FIRST VOICE
And Willy Nilly, rumbling, jockeys out again to the three-seated shack called the House of Commons in the back where the hens weep, and sees, in sudden Springshine,

SECOND VOICE
herring gulls heckling down to the harbour where the fishermen spit and prop the morning up and eye the fishy sea smooth to the sea's end as it lulls in blue. Green and gold money, tobacco, tinned salmon, hats with feathers, pots of fish-paste, warmth for the winter-to-be, weave and leap in it rich and slippery in the flash and shapes of fishes through the cold sea-streets. But with blue lazy eyes the fishermen gaze at that milk-mild whispering water with no ruck or ripple as though it blew great guns and serpents and typhooned the town.

FISHERMAN
Too rough for fishing to-day.

SECOND VOICE
And they thank God, and gob at a gull for luck, and moss-slow and silent make their way uphill, from the still still sea, towards the Sailors Arms as the children     [*School bell*

FIRST VOICE
spank and scamper rough and singing out of school into the draggletail yard. And Captain Cat at his window says soft to himself the words of their song.

CAPTAIN CAT (*To the beat of the singing*)
Johnnie Crack and Flossie Snail
Kept their baby in a milking pail
Flossie Snail and Johnnie Crack
One would pull it out and one would put it back

O it's my turn now said Flossie Snail
To take the baby from the milking pail
And it's my turn now said Johnnie Crack

[42]

To smack it on the head and put it back
Johnnie Crack and Flossie Snail
Kept their baby in a milking pail
One would put it back and one would pull it out
And all it had to drink was ale and stout
For Johnnie Crack and Flossie Snail
Always used to say that stout and ale
Was *good* for a baby in a milking pail.                    [*Long pause*

FIRST VOICE
The music of the spheres is heard distinctly over Milk Wood.
It is 'The Rustle of Spring'.

SECOND VOICE
A glee-party sings in Bethesda Graveyard, gay but muffled.

FIRST VOICE
Vegetables make love above the tenors

SECOND VOICE
and dogs bark blue in the face.

FIRST VOICE
Mrs Ogmore-Pritchard belches in a teeny hanky and chases
the sunlight with a flywhisk, but even she cannot drive out
the Spring: from one of the finger-bowls a primrose grows.

SECOND VOICE
Mrs Dai Bread One and Mrs Dai Bread Two are sitting
outside their house in Donkey Lane, one darkly one plumply
blooming in the quick, dewy sun. Mrs Dai Bread Two is
looking into a crystal ball which she holds in the lap of her
dirty yellow petticoat, hard against her hard dark thighs.

MRS DAI BREAD TWO
Cross my palm with silver. Out of our housekeeping money.
Aah!

MRS DAI BREAD ONE
What d'you see, lovie?

MRS DAI BREAD TWO
I see a featherbed. With three pillows on it. And a text above
the bed. I can't read what it says, there's great clouds
blowing. Now they have blown away. God is Love, the text
says.

MRS DAI BREAD ONE (*Delighted*)
That's *our* bed.

MRS DAI BREAD TWO
And now it's vanished. The sun's spinning like a top. Who's
this coming out of the sun? It's a hairy little man with big
pink lips. He got a wall eye.

[43]

MRS DAI BREAD ONE
  It's Dai, it's Dai Bread!

MRS DAI BREAD TWO
  Ssh! The featherbed's floating back. The little man's taking
  his boots off. He's pulling his shirt over his head. He's
  beating his chest with his fists. He's climbing into bed.

MRS DAI BREAD ONE
  Go on, go on.

MRS DAI BREAD TWO
  There's *two* women in bed. He looks at them both, with his
  head cocked on one side. He's whistling through his teeth.
  Now he grips his little arms round one of the women.

MRS DAI BREAD ONE
  Which one, which one?

MRS DAI BREAD TWO
  I can't see any more. There's great clouds blowing again.

MRS DAI BREAD ONE
  Ach, the mean old clouds!
                    [*Pause. The children's singing fades*

FIRST VOICE
  The morning is all singing. The Reverend Eli Jenkins, busy
  on his morning calls, stops outside the Welfare Hall to hear
  Polly Garter as she scrubs the floors for the Mothers' Union
  Dance to-night.

POLLY GARTER (*Singing*)
  I loved a man whose name was Tom
  He was strong as a bear and two yards long
  I loved a man whose name was Dick
  He was big as a barrel and three feet thick
  And I loved a man whose name was Harry
  Six feet tall and sweet as a cherry
  But the one I loved best awake or asleep
  Was little Willy Wee and he's six feet deep.

  O Tom Dick and Harry were three fine men
  And I'll never have such loving again
  But little Willy Wee who took me on his knee
  Little Willy Wee was the man for me.

  Now men from every parish round
  Run after me and roll me on the ground
  But whenever I love another man back
  Johnnie from the Hill or Sailing Jack
  I always think as they do what they please

Of Tom Dick and Harry who were tall as trees
And most I think when I'm by their side
Of little Willy Wee who downed and died.

O Tom Dick and Harry were three fine men
And I'll never have such loving again
But little Willy Wee who took me on his knee
Little Willy Weazel is the man for me.

REV. ELI JENKINS
Praise the Lord! We are a musical nation.

SECOND VOICE
And the Reverend Jenkins hurries on through the town to
visit the sick with jelly and poems.

FIRST VOICE
The town's as full as a lovebird's egg.

MR WALDO
There goes the Reverend,

FIRST VOICE
says Mr Waldo at the smoked herring brown window of the
unwashed Sailors Arms,

MR WALDO
with his brolly and his odes. Fill 'em up, Sinbad, I'm on the
treacle to-day.

SECOND VOICE
The silent fishermen flush down their pints.

SINBAD
Oh, Mr Waldo,

FIRST VOICE
sighs Sinbad Sailors,

SINBAD
I dote on that Gossamer Beynon. She's a lady all over.

FIRST VOICE
And Mr Waldo, who is thinking of a woman soft as Eve and
sharp as sciatica to share his bread-pudding bed, answers

MR WALDO
No lady that I know is.

SINBAD
And if only grandma'd die, cross my heart I'd go down on my
knees Mr Waldo and I'd say Miss Gossamer I'd say

CHILDREN'S VOICES
When birds do sing hey ding a ding a ding
Sweet lovers love the Spring . . .

[45]

SECOND VOICE
  Polly Garter sings, still on her knees,

POLLY GARTER
  Tom Dick and Harry were three fine men
  And I'll never have such

CHILDREN
  ding a ding

POLLY GARTER
  again.

FIRST VOICE
  And the morning school is over, and Captain Cat at his
  curtained schooner's porthole open to the Spring sun tides
  hears the naughty forfeiting children tumble and rhyme on
  the cobbles.

GIRLS' VOICES
  Gwennie call the boys
  They make such a noise.

GIRL
  Boys boys boys
  Come along to me.

GIRLS' VOICES
  Boys boys boys
  Kiss Gwennie where she says
  Or give her a penny.
  Go on, Gwennie.

GIRL
  Kiss me in Goosegog Lane
  Or give me a penny.
  What's your name?

FIRST BOY
  Billy.

GIRL
  Kiss me in Goosegog Lane Billy
  Or give me a penny silly.

FIRST BOY
  Gwennie Gwennie
  I kiss you in Goosegog Lane.
  Now I haven't got to give you a penny.

GIRL'S VOICES
  Boys boys boys
  Kiss Gwennie where she says
  Or give her a penny.
  Go on, Gwennie.

[46]

**GIRL**

    Kiss me on Llareggub Hill
    Or give me a penny.
    What's your name?

**SECOND BOY**

    Johnnie Cristo.

**GIRL**

    Kiss me on Llareggub Hill Johnnie Cristo
    Or give me a penny mister.

**SECOND BOY**

    Gwennie Gwennie
    I kiss you on Llareggub Hill.
    Now I haven't got to give you a penny.

**GIRLS' VOICES**

    Boys boys boys
    Kiss Gwennie where she says
    Or give her a penny.
    Go on, Gwennie.

**GIRL**

    Kiss me in Milk Wood
    Or give me a penny.
    What's your name?

**THIRD BOY**

    Dicky.

**GIRL**

    Kiss me in Milk Wood Dicky
    Or give me a penny quickly.

**THIRD BOY**

    Gwennie Gwennie
    I can't kiss you in Milk Wood.

**GIRLS' VOICES**

    Gwennie ask him why.

**GIRL**

    Why?

**THIRD BOY**

    Because my mother says I mustn't.

**GIRLS' VOICES**

    Cowardy cowardy custard
    Give Gwennie a penny.

**GIRL**

    Give me a penny.

THIRD BOY
I haven't got any.

GIRLS' VOICES
Put him in the river
Up to his liver
Quick quick Dirty Dick
Beat him on the bum
With a rhubarb stick.
Aiee!
Hush!

FIRST VOICE
And the shrill girls giggle and master around him and squeal
as they clutch and thrash, and he blubbers away downhill
with his patched pants falling, and his tear-splashed blush
burns all the way as the triumphant bird-like sisters scream
with buttons in their claws and the bully brothers hoot after
him his little nickname and his mother's shame and his
father's wickedness with the loose wild barefoot women of
the hovels of the hills. It all means nothing at all, and,
howling for his milky mum, for her cawl and buttermilk and
cowbreath and welshcakes and the fat birth-smelling bed
and moonlit kitchen of her arms, he'll never forget as he
paddles blind home through the weeping end of the world.
Then his tormentors tussle and run to the Cockle Street
sweet-shop, their pennies sticky as honey, to buy from Miss
Myfanwy Price, who is cocky and neat as a puff-bosomed
robin and her small round buttocks tight as ticks, gobstoppers
big as wens that rainbow as you suck, brandyballs,
winegums, hundreds and thousands, liquorice sweet as sick,
nougat to tug and ribbon out like another red rubbery
tongue, gum to glue in girls' curls, crimson coughdrops to
spit blood, ice-cream cornets, dandelion-and-burdock,
raspberry and cherryade, pop goes the weasel and the wind.

SECOND VOICE
Gossamer Beynon high-heels out of school. The sun hums
down through the cotton flowers of her dress into the bell of
her heart and buzzes in the honey there and couches and
kisses, lazy-loving and boozed, in her red-berried breast.
Eyes run from the trees and windows of the street, steaming
'Gossamer', and strip her to the nipples and the bees. She
blazes naked past the Sailors Arms, the only woman on the
Dai-Adamed earth. Sinbad Sailors places on her thighs still
dewdamp from the first mangrowing cock-crow garden his
reverent goat-bearded hands.

GOSSAMER BEYNON
I don't care if he *is* common,

SECOND VOICE

she whispers to her salad-day deep self,

GOSSAMER BEYNON

I want to gobble him up. I don't care if he *does* drop his aitches,

SECOND VOICE

she tells the stripped and mother-of-the-world big-beamed and Eve-hipped spring of her self,

GOSSAMER BEYNON

so long as he's all cucumber and hooves.

SECOND VOICE

Sinbad Sailors watches her go by, demure and proud and schoolmarm in her crisp flower dress and sun-defying hat, with never a look or lilt or wriggle, the butcher's unmelting icemaiden daughter veiled for ever from the hungry hug of his eyes.

SINBAD SAILORS

Oh, Gossamer Beynon, why are you so proud?

SECOND VOICE

he grieves to his guinness,

SINBAD SAILORS

Oh, beautiful beautiful Gossamer B, I wish I wish that you were for me. I wish you were not so educated.

SECOND VOICE

She feels his goatbeard tickle her in the middle of the world like a tuft of wiry fire, and she turns in a terror of delight away from his whips and whiskery conflagration, and sits down in the kitchen to a plate heaped high with chips and the kidneys of lambs.

FIRST VOICE

In the blind-drawn dark dining-room of School House, dusty and echoing as a dining-room in a vault, Mr and Mrs Pugh are silent over cold grey cottage pie. Mr Pugh reads, as he forks the shroud meat in, from *Lives of the Great Poisoners*. He has bound a plain brown-paper cover round the book. Slyly, between slow mouthfuls, he sidespies up at Mrs Pugh, poisons her with his eye, then goes on reading. He underlines certain passages and smiles in secret.

MRS PUGH

Persons with manners do not read at table,

FIRST VOICE

says Mrs Pugh. She swallows a digestive tablet as big as a horse-pill, washing it down with clouded peasoup water.

[*Pause*

MRS PUGH
Some persons were brought up in pigsties.

MR PUGH
Pigs don't read at table, dear.

FIRST VOICE
Bitterly she flicks dust from the broken cruet. It settles on the pie in a thin gnat-rain.

MR PUGH
Pigs can't read, my dear.

MRS PUGH
I know one who can.

FIRST VOICE
Alone in the hissing laboratory of his wishes, Mr Pugh minces among bad vats and jeroboams, tiptoes through spinneys of murdering herbs, agony dancing in his crucibles, and mixes especially for Mrs Pugh a venomous porridge unknown to toxicologists which will scald and viper through her until her ears fall off like figs, her toes grow big and black as balloons, and steam comes screaming out of her navel.

MR PUGH
You know best, dear,

FIRST VOICE
says Mr Pugh, and quick as a flash he ducks her in rat soup.

MRS PUGH
What's that book by your trough, Mr Pugh?

MR PUGH
It's a theological work, my dear. *Lives of the Great Saints.*

FIRST VOICE
Mrs Pugh smiles. An icicle forms in the cold air of the dining-vault.

MRS PUGH
I saw you talking to a saint this morning. Saint Polly Garter. She was martyred again last night. Mrs Organ Morgan saw her with Mr Waldo.

MRS ORGAN MORGAN
And when they saw me they pretended they were looking for nests,

SECOND VOICE
said Mrs Organ Morgan to her husband, with her mouth full of fish as a pelican's.

[50]

**MRS ORGAN MORGAN**

But you don't go nesting in long combinations, I said to myself, like Mr Waldo was wearing, and your dress nearly over your head like Polly Garter's. Oh, they didn't fool me.

**SECOND VOICE**

One big bird gulp, and the flounder's gone. She licks her lips and goes stabbing again.

**MRS ORGAN MORGAN**

And when you think of all those babies she's got, then all I can say is she'd better give up bird nesting that's all I can say, it isn't the right kind of hobby at all for a woman that can't say No even to midgets. Remember Bob Spit? He wasn't any bigger than a baby and he gave her two. But they're two nice boys, I will say that, Fred Spit and Arthur. Sometimes I like Fred best and sometimes I like Arthur. Who do you like best, Organ?

**ORGAN MORGAN**

Oh, Bach without any doubt. Bach every time for me.

**MRS ORGAN MORGAN**

Organ Morgan, you haven't been listening to a word I said. It's organ organ all the time with you . . .

**FIRST VOICE**

And she burst into tears, and, in the middle of her salty howling, nimbly spears a small flatfish and pelicans it whole.

**ORGAN MORGAN**

And then Palestrina,

**SECOND VOICE**

says Organ Morgan.

**FIRST VOICE**

Lord Cut-Glass, in his kitchen full of time, squats down alone to a dogdish, marked Fido, of peppery fish-scraps and listens to the voices of his sixty-six clocks, one for each year of his loony age, and watches, with love, their black-and-white moony loudlipped faces tocking the earth away: slow clocks, quick clocks, pendulumed heart-knocks, china, alarm, grandfather, cuckoo; clocks shaped like Noah's whirring Ark, clocks that bicker in marble ships, clocks in the wombs of glass women, hourglass chimers, tu-wit-tu-woo clocks, clocks that pluck tunes, Vesuvius clocks all black bells and lava, Niagara clocks that cataract their ticks, old time-weeping clocks with ebony beards, clocks with no hands for ever drumming out time without ever knowing what time it is. His sixty-six singers are all set at different hours. Lord Cut-Glass lives in a house and a life at siege. Any minute or

dark day now, the unknown enemy will loot and savage
downhill, but they will not catch him napping. Sixty-six
different times in his fish-slimy kitchen ping, strike, tick,
chime, and tock.

SECOND VOICE
The lust and lilt and lather and emerald breeze and crackle
of the bird-praise and body of Spring with its breasts full of
rivering May-milk, means, to that lordly fish-head nibbler,
nothing but another nearness to the tribes and navies of the
Last Black Day who'll sear and pillage down Armageddon
Hill to his double-locked rusty-shuttered tick-tock dust-
scrabbled shack at the bottom of the town that has fallen
head over bells in love.

POLLY GARTER
And I'll never have such loving again,

SECOND VOICE
pretty Polly hums and longs.

POLLY GARTER (*Sings*)
Now when farmers' boys on the first fair day
Come down from the hills to drink and be gay,
Before the sun sinks I'll lie there in their arms
For they're *good* bad boys from the lonely farms,

But I always think as we tumble into bed
Of little Willy Wee who is dead, dead, dead. . . .    [*A silence*

FIRST VOICE
The sunny slow lulling afternoon yawns and moons through
the dozy town. The sea lolls, laps and idles in, with fishes
sleeping in its lap. The meadows still as Sunday, the shut-eye
tasselled bulls, the goat-and-daisy dingles, nap happy and
lazy. The dumb duck-ponds snooze. Clouds sag and pillow
on Llareggub Hill. Pigs grunt in a wet wallow-bath, and
smile as they snort and dream. They dream of the acorned
swill of the world, the rooting for pig-fruit, the bagpipe dugs
of the mother sow, the squeal and snuffle of yesses of the
women pigs in rut. They mud-bask and snout in the pig-
loving sun; their tails curl; they rollick and slobber and
snore to deep, smug, after-swill sleep. Donkeys angelically
drowse on Donkey Down.

MRS PUGH
Person with manners,

SECOND VOICE
snaps Mrs cold Pugh,

MRS PUGH
do not nod at table.

FIRST VOICE
Mr Pugh cringes awake. He puts on a soft-soaping smile: it
is sad and grey under his nicotine-eggyellow weeping walrus
Victorian moustache worn thick and long in memory of
Doctor Crippen.

MRS PUGH
You should wait until you retire to your sty,

SECOND VOICE
says Mrs Pugh, sweet as a razor. His fawning measly
quarter-smile freezes. Sly and silent, he foxes into his
chemist's den and there, in a hiss and prussic circle of
cauldrons and phials brimful with pox and the Black Death,
cooks up a fricassee of deadly night-shade, nicotine, hot frog,
cyanide and bat-spit for his needling stalactite hag and
bednag of a pokerbacked nutcracker wife.

MR PUGH
I beg your pardon, my dear,

SECOND VOICE
he murmurs with a wheedle.

FIRST VOICE
Captain Cat, at his window thrown wide to the sun and the
clippered seas he sailed long ago when his eyes were blue and
bright, slumbers and voyages; ear-ringed and rolling, I Love
You Rosie Probert tattoed on his belly, he brawls with
broken bottles in the fug and babel of the dark dock bars,
roves with a herd of short and good time cows in every
naughty port and twines and souses with the drowned and
blowzy-breasted dead. He weeps as he sleeps and sails.

SECOND VOICE
One voice of all he remembers most dearly as his dream
buckets down. Lazy early Rosie with the flaxen thatch, whom
he shared with Tom-Fred the donkeyman and many another
seaman, clearly and near to him speaks from the bedroom of
her dust. In that gulf and haven, fleets by the dozen have
anchored for the little heaven of the night; but she speaks to
Captain napping Cat alone. Mrs Probert . . .

ROSIE PROBERT
from Duck Lane, Jack. Quack twice and ask for Rosie

SECOND VOICE
. . is the one love of his sea-life that was sardined with women.

ROSIE PROBERT (*Softly*)
What seas did you see,
Tom Cat, Tom Cat,

In your sailoring days
Long long ago?
What sea beasts were
In the wavery green
When you were my master?

CAPTAIN CAT
I'll tell you the truth.
Seas barking like seals,
Blue seas and green,
Seas covered with eels
And mermen and whales.

ROSIE PROBERT
What seas did you sail
Old whaler when
On the blubbery waves
Between Frisco and Wales
You were my bosun?

CAPTAIN CAT
As true as I'm here
Dear you Tom Cat's tart
You landlubber Rosie
You cosy love
My easy as easy
My true sweetheart,
Seas green as a bean
Seas gliding with swans
In the seal-barking moon.

ROSIE PROBERT
What seas were rocking
My little deck hand
My favourite husband
In your seaboots and hunger
My duck my whaler
My honey my daddy
My pretty sugar sailor.
With my name on your belly
When you were a boy
Long long ago?

CAPTAIN CAT
I'll tell you no lies.
The only sea I saw
Was the seesaw sea
With you riding on it.
Lie down, lie easy.
Let me shipwreck in your thighs.

ROSIE PROBERT
  Knock twice, Jack,
  At the door of my grave
  And ask for Rosie.

CAPTAIN CAT
  Rosie Probert.

ROSIE PROBERT
  Remember her.
  She is forgetting.
  The earth which filled her mouth
  Is vanishing from her.
  Remember me.
  I have forgotten you.
  I am going into the darkness of the darkness for ever.
  I have forgotten that I was ever born.

CHILD
  Look,

FIRST VOICE
  says a child to her mother as they pass by the window of
  Schooner House,

CHILD
  Captain Cat is crying

FIRST VOICE
  Captain Cat is crying

CAPTAIN CAT
  Come back, come back,

FIRST VOICE
  up the silences and echoes of the passages of the eternal night.

CHILD
  He's crying all over his nose,

FIRST VOICE
  says the child. Mother and child move on down the street.

CHILD
  He's got a nose like strawberries,

FIRST VOICE
  the child says; and then she forgets him too. She sees in the
  still middle of the bluebagged bay Nogood Boyo fishing
  from the *Zanzibar*.

CHILD
  Nogood Boyo gave me three pennies yesterday but I
  wouldn't,

FIRST VOICE
the child tells her mother.

SECOND VOICE
Boyo catches a whalebone corset. It is all he has caught all day.

NOGOOD BOYO
Bloody funny fish!

SECOND VOICE
Mrs Dai Bread Two gypsies up his mind's slow eye, dressed only in a bangle.

NOGOOD BOYO
She's wearing her nightgown. (*Pleadingly*) Would you like this nice wet corset, Mrs Dai Bread Two?

MRS DAI BREAD TWO
No, I *won't*!

NOGOOD BOYO
And a bite of my little apple?

SECOND VOICE
he offers with no hope.

FIRST VOICE
She shakes her brass nightgown, and he chases her out of his mind; and when he comes gusting back, there in the bloodshot centre of his eye a geisha girl grins and bows in a kimono of ricepaper.

NOGOOD BOYO
I want to be *good* Boyo, but nobody'll let me,

FIRST VOICE
he sighs as she writhes politely. The land fades, the sea flocks silently away; and through the warm white cloud where he lies, silky, tingling, uneasy Eastern music undoes him in a Japanese minute.

SECOND VOICE
The afternoon buzzes like lazy bees round the flowers round Mae Rose Cottage. Nearly asleep in the field of nannygoats who hum and gently butt the sun, she blows love on a puffball.

MAE ROSE COTTAGE (*Lazily*)
He loves me
He loves me not
He loves me
He loves me not
He *loves* me!—the dirty old fool.

SECOND VOICE
Lazy she lies alone in clover and sweet-grass, seventeen and never been sweet in the grass ho ho.

FIRST VOICE
The Reverend Eli Jenkins inky in his cool front parlour or poem-room tells only the truth in his Lifework—the Population, Main Industry, Shipping, History, Topography, Flora and Fauna of the town he worships in—the White Book of Llareggub. Portraits of famous bards and preachers, all fur and wool from the squint to the kneecaps, hang over him heavy as sheep, next to faint lady watercolours of pale green Milk Wood like a lettuce salad dying. His mother, propped against a pot in a palm, with her wedding-ring waist and bust like a black-clothed dining-table suffers in her stays.

REV. ELI JENKINS
Oh angels be careful there with your knives and forks,

FIRST VOICE
he prays. There is no known likeness of his father Esau, who, undogcollared because of his little weakness, was scythed to the bone one harvest by mistake when sleeping with his weakness in the corn. He lost all ambition and died, with one leg.

REV. ELI JENKINS
Poor Dad,

SECOND VOICE
grieves the Reverend Eli,

REV. ELI JENKINS
to die of drink and agriculture.

SECOND VOICE
Farmer Watkins in Salt Lake Farm hates his cattle on the hill as he ho's them in to milking.

UTAH WATKINS (*In a fury*)
Damn you, you damned dairies!

SECOND VOICE
A cow kisses him.

UTAH WATKINS
Bite her to death!

SECOND VOICE
he shouts to his deaf dog who smiles and licks his hands.

UTAH WATKINS
Gore him, sit on him, Daisy!

he bawls to the cow who barbed him with her tongue,
and she moos gentle words as he raves and dances among his
summerbreathed slaves walking delicately to the farm. The
coming of the end of the Spring day is already reflected in
the lakes of their great eyes. Bessie Bighead greets them by
the names she gave them when they were maidens.

BESSIE BIGHEAD
Peg, Meg, Buttercup, Moll,
Fan from the Castle,
Theodosia and Daisy.

SECOND VOICE
They bow their heads.

FIRST VOICE
Look up Bessie Bighead in the White Book of Llareggub
and you will find the few haggard rags and the one poor
glittering thread of her history laid out in pages there with as
much love and care as the lock of hair of a first lost love.
Conceived in Milk Wood, born in a barn, wrapped in paper,
left on a doorstep, big-headed and bass-voiced she grew in
the dark until long-dead Gomer Owen kissed her when she
wasn't looking because he was dared. Now in the light she'll
work, sing, milk, say the cows' sweet names and sleep until
the night sucks out her soul and spits it into the sky. In her
life-long love light, holily Bessie milks the fond lake-eyed
cows as dusk showers slowly down over byre, sea and town.
Utah Watkins curses through the farmyard on a carthorse.

UTAH WATKINS
Gallop, you bleeding cripple!

FIRST VOICE
and the huge horse neighs softly as though he had given it a
lump of sugar.
    Now the town is dusk. Each cobble, donkey, goose and
gooseberry street is a thoroughfare of dusk; and dusk and
ceremonial dust, and night's first darkening snow, and the
sleep of birds, drift under and through the live dusk of this
place of love. Llareggub is the capital of dusk.
    Mrs Ogmore-Pritchard, at the first drop of the dusk-shower,
seals all her sea-view doors, draws the germ-free blinds, sits,
erect as a dry dream on a high-backed hygienic chair and
wills herself to cold, quick sleep. At once, at twice, Mr
Ogmore and Mr Pritchard, who all dead day long have been
gossiping like ghosts in the woodshed, planning the loveless
destruction of their glass widow, reluctantly sigh and sidle
into her clean house.

**MR PRITCHARD**
You first, Mr Ogmore.

**MR OGMORE**
After you, Mr Pritchard.

**MR PRITCHARD**
No, no, Mr Ogmore. You widowed her first.

**FIRST VOICE**
And in through the keyhole, with tears where their eyes
once were, they ooze and grumble.

**MRS OGMORE-PRITCHARD**
Husbands,

**FIRST VOICE**
she says in her sleep. There is acid love in her voice for one
of the two shambling phantoms. Mr Ogmore hopes that it is
not for him. So does Mr Pritchard.

**MRS OGMORE-PRITCHARD**
I love you both.

**MR OGMORE** (*With terror*)
Oh, Mrs Ogmore.

**MR PRITCHARD** (*With horror*)
Oh, Mrs Pritchard.

**MRS OGMORE-PRITCHARD**
Soon it will be time to go to bed. Tell me your tasks in order.

**MR OGMORE AND MR PRITCHARD**
We must take our pyjamas from the drawer marked pyjamas.

**MRS OGMORE-PRITCHARD** (*Coldly*)
And then you must take them off.

**SECOND VOICE**
Down in the dusking town, Mae Rose Cottage, still lying in
clover, listens to the nannygoats chew, draws circles of
lipstick round her nipples.

**MAE ROSE COTTAGE**
I'm *fast*. I'm a bad lot. God will strike me dead. I'm
seventeen. I'll go to hell,

**SECOND VOICE**
she tells the goats.

**MAE ROSE COTTAGE**
You just wait. I'll sin till I blow up!

**SECOND VOICE**
She lies deep, waiting for the worst to happen; the goats
champ and sneer.

FIRST VOICE
And at the doorway of Bethesda House, the Reverend
Jenkins recites to Llareggub Hill his sunset poem.

REV. ELI JENKINS
Every morning when I wake,
Dear Lord, a little prayer I make,
O please to keep Thy lovely eye
On all poor creatures born to die.

And every evening at sun-down
I ask a blessing on the town,
For whether we last the night or no
I'm sure is always touch-and-go.

We are not wholly bad or good
Who live our lives under Milk Wood,
And Thou, I know, wilt be the first
To see our best side, not our worst.

O let us see another day!
Bless us this night, I pray,
And to the sun we all will bow
And say, good-bye—but just for now!

FIRST VOICE
Jack Black prepares once more to meet his Satan in the
Wood. He grinds his night-teeth, closes his eyes, climbs into
his religious trousers, their flies sewn up with cobbler's
thread, and pads out, torched and bibled, grimly, joyfully,
into the already sinning dusk.

JACK BLACK
Off to Gomorrah!

SECOND VOICE
And Lily Smalls is up to Nogood Boyo in the wash-house.

FIRST VOICE
And Cherry Owen, sober as Sunday as he is every day of the
week, goes off happy as Saturday to get drunk as a deacon as
he does every night.

CHERRY OWEN
I always say she's got two husbands,

FIRST VOICE
says Cherry Owen,

CHERRY OWEN
one drunk and one sober.

FIRST VOICE
And Mrs Cherry simply says

MRS CHERRY OWEN
   And aren't I a lucky woman? Because I love them both.

SINBAD
   Evening, Cherry.

CHERRY OWEN
   Evening, Sinbad.

SINBAD
   What'll you have?

CHERRY OWEN
   Too much.

SINBAD
   The Sailors Arms is always open . . .

FIRST VOICE
   Sinbad suffers to himself, heartbroken,

SINBAD
   . . . oh, Gossamer, open yours!

FIRST VOICE
   Dusk is drowned for ever until to-morrow. It is all at once
   night now. The windy town is a hill of windows, and from
   the larrupped waves the lights of the lamps in the windows
   call back the day and the dead that have run away to sea. All
   over the calling dark, babies and old men are bribed and
   lullabied to sleep.

FIRST WOMAN'S VOICE
   Hushabye, baby, the sandman is coming . . .

SECOND WOMAN'S VOICE (*Singing*)
   Rockabye, grandpa, in the tree top,
   When the wind blows the cradle will rock,
   When the bough breaks the cradle will fall,
   Down will come grandpa, whiskers and all.

FIRST VOICE
   Or their daughters cover up the old unwinking men like
   parrots, and in their little dark in the lit and bustling young
   kitchen corners, all night long they watch, beady-eyed, the
   long night through in case death catches them asleep.

SECOND VOICE
   Unmarried girls, alone in their privately bridal bedrooms,
   powder and curl for the Dance of the World.
                                      [*Accordion music: dim*

     They make, in front of their looking-glasses, haughty or
   come-hithering faces for the young men in the street outside,

at the lamplit leaning corners, who wait in the all-at-once wind to wolve and whistle.

[*Accordion music louder, then fading under*

FIRST VOICE
The drinkers in the Sailors Arms drink to the failure of the dance.

A DRINKER
Down with the waltzing and the skipping.

CHERRY OWEN
Dancing isn't natural,

FIRST VOICE
righteously says Cherry Owen who has just downed seventeen pints of flat, warm, thin, Welsh, bitter beer.

SECOND VOICE
A farmer's lantern glimmers, a spark on Llareggub hillside.

[*Accordion music fades into silence*

FIRST VOICE
Llareggub Hill, writes the Reverend Jenkins in his poem-room,

REV. ELI JENKINS
Llareggub Hill, that mystic tumulus, the memorial of peoples that dwelt in the region of Llareggub before the Celts left the Land of Summer and where the old wizards made themselves a wife out of flowers.

SECOND VOICE
Mr Waldo, in his corner of the Sailors Arms, sings:

MR WALDO
In Pembroke City when I was young
I lived by the Castle Keep
Sixpence a week was my wages
For working for the chimbley-sweep.
Six cold pennies he gave me
Not a farthing more or less
And all the fare I could afford
Was parsnip gin and watercress.
I did not need a knife and fork
Or a bib up to my chin
To dine on a dish of watercress
And a jug of parsnip gin.
Did you ever hear a growing boy
To live so cruel cheap
On grub that has no flesh and bones
And liquor that makes you weep?
Sweep sweep chimbley sweep,

I wept through Pembroke City
Poor and barefoot in the snow
Till a kind young woman took pity.
Poor little chimbley sweep she said
Black as the ace of spades
O nobody's swept my chimbley
Since my husband went his ways.
Come and sweep my chimbley
Come and sweep my chimbley
She sighed to me with a blush
Come and sweep my chimbley
Come and sweep my chimbley
Bring along your chimbley brush!

FIRST VOICE
Blind Captain Cat climbs into his bunk. Like a cat, he sees in the dark. Through the voyages of his tears he sails to see the dead.

CAPTAIN CAT
Dancing Williams!

FIRST DROWNED
Still dancing.

CAPTAIN CAT
Jonah Jarvis

THIRD DROWNED
Still.

FIRST DROWNED
Curly Bevan's skull.

ROSIE PROBERT
Rosie, with God. She has forgotten dying.

FIRST VOICE
The dead come out in their Sunday best.

SECOND VOICE
Listen to the night breaking.

FIRST VOICE
Organ Morgan goes to chapel to play the organ. He sees Bach lying on a tombstone.

ORGAN MORGAN
Johann Sebastian!

CHERRY OWEN (*Drunkenly*)
Who?

[63]

ORGAN MORGAN
  Johann Sebastian mighty Bach. Oh, Bach fach.

CHERRY OWEN
  To hell with you,

FIRST VOICE
  says Cherry Owen who is resting on the tombstone on his
  way home.
    Mr Mog Edwards and Miss Myfanwy Price happily apart
  from one another at the top and the sea end of the town
  write their everynight letters of love and desire. In the warm
  White Book of Llareggub you will find the little maps of
  the islands of their contentment.

MYFANWY PRICE
  Oh, my Mog, I am yours for ever.

FIRST VOICE
  And she looks around with pleasure at her own neat
  neverdull room which Mr Mog Edwards will never enter.

MOG EDWARDS
  Come to my arms, Myfanwy.

FIRST VOICE
  And he hugs his lovely money to his *own* heart.
    And Mr Waldo drunk in the dusky wood hugs his lovely
  Polly Garter under the eyes and rattling tongues of the
  neighbours and the birds, and he does not care. He smacks
  his live red lips.
    But it is not *his* name that Polly Garter whispers as she lies
  under the oak and loves him back. Six feet deep that name
  sings in the cold earth.

POLLY GARTER (*Sings*)
  But I always think as we tumble into bed
  Of little Willy Wee who is dead, dead, dead.

FIRST VOICE
  The thin night darkens. A breeze from the creased water
  sighs the streets close under Milk waking Wood. The Wood,
  whose every tree-foot's cloven in the black glad sight of the
  hunters of lovers, that is a God-built garden to Mary Ann
  Sailors who knows there is Heaven on earth and the chosen
  people of His kind fire in Llareggub's land, that is the fairday
  farmhands' wantoning ignorant chapel of bridesbeds, and, to
  the Reverend Eli Jenkins, a greenleaved sermon on the
  innocence of men, the suddenly wind-shaken wood springs
  awake for the second dark time this one Spring day.

[64]